DATE DUE			

2008 UNITED STATES DEMOCRATIC PARTY PRESIDENTIAL CANDIDATES

The Historic Fight for the 2008 Democratic Presidential Nomination

THE CLINTON VIEW

Hillary Clinton's run for president inspired young girls across the country to get involved with the election.

Mitchell Lane

PUBLISHERS

P.O. Box 196

Hockessin, Delaware 19707

**The
Clinton View**

Clinton's 2008 Election Platform on . . .

Economy Protect the next generation by paying off the United States' debt; reduce outsourcing—bring more jobs back home; reduce taxes within a balanced budget

Foreign Policy Fight terrorism with cooperation; become more engaged in world affairs involving human rights; lead by staying engaged with the rest of the world

Health Care Support universal health care; increase the commitment to the Global AIDS crisis; implement high penalties for underage smoking; strengthen the Medicare program

Homeland Security Support a nuclear test ban treaty; reauthorize the Patriot Act (excluding the wiretap provision)

**The
Obama View**

Obama's 2008 Election Platform on . . .

Economy Provide a tax cut for working families; provide tax relief for small businesses and startups; fight for fair trade

Foreign Policy Secure loose nuclear materials from terrorists; pursue tough, direct diplomacy without preconditions to end the threat from Iran; renew American diplomacy

Health Care Make health insurance affordable and accessible to all; lower health care costs; promote public health

Homeland Security Defeat terrorism worldwide; prevent nuclear terrorism; strengthen American biosecurity

2008 UNITED STATES DEMOCRATIC PARTY PRESIDENTIAL CANDIDATES

The Historic Fight for the 2008 Democratic Presidential Nomination

THE CLINTON VIEW

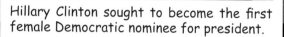

Hillary Clinton sought to become the first female Democratic nominee for president.

Kathleen Tracy

Mitchell Lane

PUBLISHERS

Copyright © 2009 by Mitchell Lane Publishers, Inc. All rights reserved. No part of this book may be reproduced without written permission from the publisher. Printed and bound in the United States of America.

Printing   1   2   3   4   5   6   7   8   9

Library of Congress Cataloging-in-Publication Data
Tracy, Kathleen.
  The historic fight for the 2008 Democratic presidential nomination : the Clinton view / by Kathleen Tracy.
     p. cm. — (Monumental milestones)
  Includes bibliographical references and index.
  ISBN 978-1-58415-731-1 (library bound)
  1. Clinton, Hillary Rodham—Juvenile literature. 2. Women presidential candidates—United States—Biography—Juvenile literature. 3. Presidential candidates—United States—Biography—Juvenile literature. 4. Presidents—United States—Election—2008—Juvenile literature. 5. Women legislators—United States—Biography—Juvenile literature. 6. United States. Congress. Senate—Biography—Juvenile literature. 7. Presidents' spouses—United States—Biography—Juvenile literature. I. Title.
  E887.C55T73 2009
  973.931092—dc22
  [B]
                                                                    2008053545

ABOUT THE AUTHOR: Kathleen Tracy has been a journalist for over twenty years. Her writing has been featured in magazines including *The Toronto Star's* "Star Week," *A&E Biography* magazine, *KidScreen* and *TV Times*. She is also the author of numerous books for Mitchell Lane Publishers, including *William Hewlett: Pioneer of the Computer Age; The Fall of the Berlin Wall; Leonardo da Vinci; Odysseus; The McCarthy Era; The Life and Times of Rosa Parks; Johnny Depp; Mariah Carey;* and *Kelly Clarkson.*

PUBLISHER'S NOTE: This story is based on the author's extensive research, which she believes to be accurate. Documentation of such research is on page 46.

The internet sites referenced herein were active as of the publication date. Due to the fleeting nature of some web sites, we cannot guarantee they will all be active when you are reading this book.

★

The Historic Fight for the 2008 Democratic Presidential Nomination

THE CLINTON VIEW

Contents

*For Your Information

In her campaign, Clinton called for Americans to cut their consumption of foreign oil in half by 2025 and increase investment in alternative energy research and individual responsibility.

If elected president, she promised to support wind and solar energy and to promote higher fuel-efficiency standards.

The Comeback Kid

The 1990s had been a time of prosperity and confidence in America. One of President William Jefferson "Bill" Clinton's most impressive domestic economic achievements was to erase the national deficit, or government debt, and turn it into a surplus. The healthy economy created jobs, and most citizens were able to afford to buy cars and homes and send their kids to college.

But by 2007, the nation's economy was struggling. Prices for basic necessities such as food and gasoline had skyrocketed. Many companies were closing or cutting their workforce, so more people were unemployed. House values started to fall, leaving many people owing the bank more money than the house was worth. It was a time of worry and fear—would the economy get worse before it got better?

As America prepared to select a new president in 2008, many citizens wanted the next administration to be completely different from that of Republican President George W. Bush, who had been in office since 2000. That desire for a new kind of leadership would lead to a historic race for the Democratic nomination, one that pitted a female candidate against an African American. Whoever won the Democratic primary would make history and, if he or she went on to become president, have the chance to change the face of American politics.

Even before she officially announced her candidacy for president of the United States, Hillary Rodham Clinton was the favorite to win the Democratic nomination. In late 2007, national polls put her thirty percentage points ahead of her closest rival, Barack Obama. Her strategy at the time was to concentrate on securing the larger, delegate-rich states while Obama focused on Iowa—the first state to allot their delegates for election caucuses. Results in Iowa receive

Clinton stressed that the middle class is the backbone of the U.S. economy.

If elected president, she promised to seek double funding for job training, to scale back tax breaks for the richest Americans, to promote public works jobs that would modernize cities' infrastructures, and to renovate public buildings to make them green.

a huge amount of media coverage, and many believe that they can sway an election.

As the date of the Iowa caucuses approached (January 3), not only had Clinton's lead vanished, it was clear her campaign was faltering. Voters were swayed by Obama's message about change and his characterization of Clinton as a typical Washington insider committed to politics as usual. Clinton shifted into damage control, crisscrossing the state in hopes of connecting with Iowa voters. She also defended herself against Obama's charges that she was taking credit for the successes of her husband, former president Bill Clinton, without acceptable culpability for his administration's failures.

"Well, I understand the point, but it's, it's really beside the point," Clinton said. "I have been very forthright in saying that we weren't successful on health care. The whole world saw that. But I think you know more about someone by seeing how they respond to setbacks than successes."

Clinton believed if given the chance, she could connect with undecided voters. "In New York, I could meet enough people, I could have a ripple effect of friends talking to friends and family talking to family and, pretty soon, a lot of people creating a critical mass could say, *Hey, I met her. I got to know her. She's not as bad as I thought.*"[1]

Her efforts came up short. Clinton took a humbling third place in the Iowa caucuses, behind Obama and former senator John Edwards, and suddenly there were suggestions from some conservative political pundits that Obama's surging popularity sounded the end for Clinton's run for the presidency. And many in the press crowned Obama the new front-runner.

Officials in Clinton's campaign were upset over what they felt was unbalanced media coverage of the candidates. Media analyst Howard Kurtz of the *Washington Post* investigated the claim and found several reporters agreed.

"She's just held to a different standard in every respect," said Mark Halperin, *Time*'s editor at large. While he agreed that Clinton's mistakes deserved full coverage, he added that "the press's flaws—wild swings, accentuating the negative—are magnified 50 times when it comes to her. It's not a level playing field. . . .

"Your typical reporter has a thinly disguised preference that Barack Obama be the nominee. The narrative of him beating her is better than her beating him, in part because she's a Clinton and in part because he's a young African American. . . . There's no one rooting for her to come back."[2]

Neutrality, a foundation of balanced journalism, often went out the window, such as when MSNBC commentator Chris Matthews openly supported Obama as a candidate. *Newsweek*'s Howard Fineman observed that the press was more excited about Obama. "While they don't say so publicly because it's risky to complain, a lot of operatives from other campaigns say he's getting a free ride, that people aren't tough enough on Obama," Fineman noted. "There may be something to that. He's the new guy, an interesting guy, a pathbreaker and trendsetter perhaps."[3]

NBC's Brian Williams raised some eyebrows when he reported that his network's correspondent covering Obama admitted it was hard to be objective covering the Illinois senator. *Politico* observed that many journalists were also enamored with Republican candidate John McCain because of the access he gave them. "Hillary Clinton, cautious and scripted, got the reverse treatment. She is carrying the burden of 16 years of contentious relations between the Clintons and the news media."[4]

The public was inclined to agree. In a *New York Times*/CBS News poll published January 14, 2008, fifty-one percent of Democratic primary voters, especially women, believed the media had been harsher with Clinton than with any of the other candidates. Only 12 percent thought the media had been harder on Obama.

As the New Hampshire primary approached, it seemed as if Clinton's campaign might suffer a stunning early derailment. Polls consistently showed Obama ahead, and he seemed more confident and self-assured each day. Some of Clinton's advisers were privately urging her to show more emotion and passion in an attempt to humanize her and to counterbalance the image of the calculating politician frequently painted of her by the media.

The strain of being behind in the polls and trying to salvage her campaign eventually caught up with her. The day before the New Hampshire primary, Clinton was asked how she coped, and she appeared uncharacteristically vulnerable. "It's not easy," she admitted, teary-eyed. "This is very personal for me. It's not just political. It's not just public. I see what's happening. And we have to reverse it. . . . I couldn't do it if I just didn't passionately believe it was the right thing to do." When asked about her uphill battle to win the primary, she said, "You know, I had so many opportunities from this country. I just don't want to see us fall backwards."[5]

To the surprise of both analysts and pollsters, Clinton won the New Hampshire primary in convincing fashion, earning 46 percent of the vote compared to Obama's 34 percent. Exit polls showed that Clinton had won with voters over 40, those without college degrees, those who made less than $50,000 a year, and women.

When Clinton appeared in front of supporters the night of the primary, she had found her political second wind. She announced: "I come tonight with a very, very full heart. And I want especially to thank New Hampshire. Over the last week, I listened to you and, in the process, I found my own voice. I felt like we all spoke from our hearts, and I am so gratified that you responded.

"I had this incredible moment of connection with the voters of New Hampshire and they saw it and they heard it," Clinton said the next day, referring to her public display of emotion prior to the election. *"And they gave me this incredible victory last night."*[6]

Clinton's come-from-behind victory in the New Hampshire primary on January 8, 2008, gave her presidential campaign a second wind.

Now, together, let's give America the kind of comeback that New Hampshire has just given me.

"For all the ups and downs of this campaign, you helped remind everyone that politics isn't a game. This campaign is about people, about making a difference in your lives, about making sure that everyone in this country has the opportunity to live up to his or her God-given potential. That has been the work of my life."[7]

She recommitted herself to her campaign and to fighting for the middle class. "We know we face challenges here at home, around the world, so many challenges for the people whose lives I've been privileged to be part of. I've met families in this state and all over our country who've lost their homes to

After her New Hampshire win, Clinton promised supporters she would stay in the race until the very end, despite Obama's momentum and huge advantage in campaign funds. She set her sights on the large swing states, intent to prove that she had more diverse and wide-ranging support.

foreclosures, men and women who work day and night but can't pay the bills and hope they don't get sick because they can't afford health insurance, young people who can't afford to go to college to pursue their dreams. Too many have been invisible for too long. Well, you are not invisible to me."[8]

Clinton had staged the unlikeliest of comebacks, vowing to stay and fight all the way to the Democratic convention in August, setting off one of the closest, hardest fought nomination races in American history. In the end, one candidate—Clinton or Obama—would make history, and supporters of the other candidate would argue that the nomination had literally been stolen from voters.

New Hampshire prides itself on being the first state to hold a presidential primary election. Although many other states would like to claim that honor, New Hampshire has steadfastly refused to relinquish its place in the election process.

Beginning in 1831, New Hampshire Democrats held caucuses to choose delegates to attend a state convention. After that year, Republicans also used that procedure for presidential elections.

In 1913, the state legislature changed its nominating system from caucuses to a primary. Delegates from each political party were listed on a statewide ballot for election to the national convention. The delegates either designated themselves as pledged to a specific candidate or as uncommitted. In 1920, two other states changed their primary dates, and by default New Hampshire found itself being the first state to hold a presidential primary for the upcoming election.

Ironically, though, no presidential candidate appeared on the state ballot. Primary voters only selected delegates to the national convention; and as a result, interest in the primary by New Hampshire voters was minimal. In 1949, Richard F. Upton, Speaker of the New Hampshire House of Representatives, came up with an idea to improve voter turnout and make the primary more meaningful to citizens. He suggested letting the voters choose named candidates directly, although initially the results were not binding. Some called it a political beauty pageant, but it brought New Hampshire national media attention. The primary results were made binding in the 1970s.

In order to safeguard its now-important position in the presidential election, New Hampshire legislators passed a law requiring the state's primary to precede that of any other's primary. (It does not count Iowa's caucus, which happens a week earlier than the New Hampshire primary.) And according to Democratic Party rules, no state can choose delegates before Iowa and New Hampshire. It is estimated that holding the first primary generates over $300 million in state revenue.

2008 New Hampshire Democratic Primary Results
22 pledged delegates, 8 unpledged

Candidate	Vote	Percentage	Delegates
Hillary Rodham Clinton	112,404	39.1%	9
Barack Obama	104,815	36.5%	9
John Edwards	48,699	16.9%	4
Bill Richardson	13,269	4.6%	0
Dennis J. Kucinich	3,891	1.4%	0
Joseph R. Biden Jr.	638	0.2%	0
Mike Gravel	404	0.1%	0
Christopher Dodd	205	0.1%	0
Others	3,217	1.1%	0

As First Lady, Clinton championed families and education, and through her efforts, the Adoption and Safe Families Act of 1997 was passed.

She also lobbied for the *Foster Care Independence bill* that would help older, unadopted children transition to adulthood.

Early Ambitions

Hillary Diane Rodham was born on October 26, 1947, in the Chicago suburb of Park Ridge, Illinois. Her father, Hugh, was a successful merchant who owned a fabric store. Her mother, Dorothy Howell, was a stay-at-home mom who had endured a difficult childhood. Dorothy's parents divorced when she was eight. Afterward, she and her younger sister were sent to live with their paternal grandparents in Los Angeles. Unhappy at having to raise their son's children, the grandparents were harsh custodians. They once made Dorothy stay in her bedroom for an entire year except for going to school—all because she was caught trick-or-treating. Dorothy moved out when she was fourteen, supporting herself by working as a nanny. She returned to Chicago a few years later, working for her mother as a housekeeper.

Hugh was a traveling salesman when he and Dorothy met. They married in 1942, and Hillary was born five years later. Two brothers followed: Hugh Jr., born in 1950, and Anthony, born in 1954. Hillary credits her mother for encouraging intellectual curiosity and instilling toughness and self-worth. Dorothy once recounted an incident from Hillary's childhood:

> We moved into this new house, new neighborhood, and she would come in crying and screaming about the fact that she'd been set upon by a group of children, mostly her age, and this one girl who was exactly her age, Suzy, across the street. . . . One day, and I said, *You know, this is just about enough, Hillary. You have to face things and show them you're not afraid.* Anyway, I said, *Just go out there and show them that you're not afraid, and if she does hit you again hit her back.*[1]

Hillary said her mother told her there was no room in their house for cowards. "She later told me she watched from behind the curtain as I squared my shoulders and marched across the street. I returned a few minutes later, glowing with victory."[2]

As a child, Hillary enjoyed sports, attended church regularly, and was a good student. She earned extra money babysitting after school and over the summers. Occasionally, she babysat the children of migrant Mexican workers. She received an early lesson in sexism and the glass ceiling when she applied to NASA and was told that girls were not accepted into the astronaut program (a policy that changed in 1978).

Her interest in politics first developed as a teenager. Ironically, she initially joined young Republican groups and in 1964 campaigned for Republican nominee Barry Goldwater, who lost to Lyndon Baines Johnson. At Wellesley, a woman's college in Massachusetts, Hillary was elected president of the campus's Young Republicans chapter. At the time, the Republican Party was not as powerfully influenced by social conservatives as it is now, and moderate-liberals had a strong voice. Hillary's main interests were civil rights and the war in Vietnam. During her junior year, she took an internship with Republican Representative Gerald Ford. By the following year, she was campaigning for Eugene McCarthy, a liberal, antiwar Democrat.

"I sometimes think that I didn't leave the Republican Party," she later commented, "as much as it left me."[3]

Hillary was also elected senior class president. During her tenure, she worked with the administration to increase African American enrollment, to grant students more freedom in choosing their courses, and to relax curfew rules for the students.

After graduating from Wellesley, she attended Yale Law School, taking internships during the summers. In 1970, she worked for the Children's Defense Fund. The following summer she was an intern on Democratic Senator Walter Mondale's subcommittee on migrant workers; and in the summer of 1972, for the campaign of Democratic presidential candidate George McGovern. Hillary was equally active at school. She served on the Board of Editors of *Yale Review of Law and Social Action,* and interned with children's advocate Marian Wright Edelman. In between all her extracurricular activities, she also met her future husband, William Jefferson Clinton, after she noticed him staring at her in the library. They were soon a couple, sharing many of the same interests and political views.

She graduated with honors in 1973, and after getting her law degree and passing the bar, Hillary was hired as a staff attorney for the Children's Defense Fund in Cambridge, Massachusetts. In the spring of 1974, during the height of the Watergate scandal, she was selected to be one of the attorneys advising the House of Representatives Judiciary Committee regarding the possible impeachment of President Richard Nixon. When Nixon resigned in August 1974, before he could be impeached, Hillary left Washington, D.C. She followed her heart—and Bill—to Arkansas, where she joined the University of Arkansas Law School faculty.

Hillary and Bill married on October 11, 1975. She kept her maiden name, mostly for professional reasons. By then Bill had already begun his political career—in 1974 he had run, unsuccessfully, for the House of Representatives. In 1976, though, he was elected Arkansas Attorney General. And in 1978, at age thirty-two, he was elected governor. His priorities were education and health, and he appointed Hillary to lead what turned out to be a successful committee on urban health care reform. In all, Bill Clinton served as Arkansas' governor for twelve years, and during that time Hillary continued to juggle public service with motherhood—their daughter Chelsea was born in 1980—and her successful, high-profile legal career. In 1988 and 1991, *The National Law Journal* named her one of the 100 most powerful lawyers in America.

When Bill Clinton was elected president in 1992 and the family moved to the White House, it was clear to everyone that Hillary was not going to be a typical First Lady . . . and that would become both her greatest strength and her Achilles heel. The vast majority of First Ladies have been homemakers. Beginning in the twentieth century, some First Ladies were professional women: Ellen Wilson was an artist, Grace Coolidge was a teacher, and Lou Henry Hoover was a geologist. While the First Lady is still expected to also be the First Hostess and be involved in causes, by and large the public expects the First Lady to stay in the background politically and not be too independent, which is one reason Hillary Rodham started using the name Hillary Clinton.

When President Clinton asked Hillary to chair the Task Force on National Health Care Reform, her visibility offended some people. She was frequently the target of harsh criticism, accused of everything from being an opportunist taking advantage of her husband's position to patronizing stay-at-home moms. Conservative talk show hosts regularly cited her lack of "family values."

Although the task force was a notable failure of the Clinton administration—it was abandoned in September 1994—Hillary continued to advocate for women's and children's causes. Her September 1995 speech at the United Nations' Fourth World Conference on Women in Beijing, which advocated the need for equal rights for women in all countries, created controversy in China. She was also one of the few public figures in the 1990s to speak out against the treatment of Afghani women by the Islamist fundamentalist Taliban government. In 1997, she successfully initiated the Children's Health Insurance Program and helped increase research funding for childhood asthma at the National Institute of Health. Her 1996 book, *It Takes a Village and Other Lessons Children Teach Us*, was a national bestseller, and Hillary donated the proceeds of her book to children's hospitals. She also received a Grammy Award for her recording of it. Meanwhile, she hosted conferences at the White House related to children's health and school violence. With Attorney General Janet Reno, she helped create the Violence Against Women office in the Department of Justice.

Although professional controversy was nothing new to Hillary during her tenure as First Lady, her most difficult time in that capacity came over a highly personal matter, when Bill admitted to having an illicit affair with White House intern Monica Lewinsky. Although there was speculation Hillary would leave the marriage and file for divorce, she defied expectations and stayed committed to her marriage, weathering the public humiliation with dignity and grace. Some political analysts believe that her handling of the Lewinsky scandal both humanized her and cemented her reputation as a person of character.

With Bill Clinton's second term coming to an end and Chelsea in college, it was Hillary's turn to pursue her own ambitions. In 1999, she announced her decision to seek the U.S. Senate seat from New York, held by Daniel Patrick Moynihan, who was retiring after four terms. Clinton beat her popular opponent, Republican Rick Lazio, by a margin of 55 to 43 percent. With her win she became the first First Lady elected to the United States Senate and the first woman elected statewide in New York.

As Hillary worked hard to represent the people of New York, she kept her political aspirations aimed much, much higher.

Thanks to role models like Hillary Clinton, today's young girls know they can grow up to be lawyers, doctors, astronauts, and senators. They can even envision a day when a woman will be president of the United States. Although in modern times these opportunities are often taken for granted, it wasn't so long ago that such dreams would have been unachievable. The political and social advances women have made in the United States are both remarkable and long overdue.

When the Puritans settled in North America, they brought with them religious customs that declared women should do whatever their husbands dictated. Even after the Revolutionary War, women were not allowed to own property individually once they were married—it automatically became the property of the husband. Women were not allowed to enter into business contracts, and getting out of an abusive marriage was impossible unless the man wanted a divorce.

Politically, treatment was equally unequal. Up until the early nineteenth century, all nationally elected officials were men. That began to change in 1916 when Jeannette Rankin, running in Montana, became the first woman elected to the U.S. Congress, winning a seat in the House of Representatives. In 1920, women finally got the right to vote, and after that more women began entering politics. In 1931, Hattie Wyatt Caraway of Arizona became the first woman elected to the U.S. Senate, winning a special election to fill the

Jeannette Rankin speaking

NATIONAL AMERICAN WOMAN SUFFRAGE ASS'N

rest of her husband's term after he died in office. Coincidentally or not, as more women assumed legislative and judicial positions, laws giving women equal property and civil rights were also enacted.

For all the advances women have made in such fields as medicine, law, manufacturing, corporate America, and the military, women would not hold high-ranking positions in the federal government until Madeleine Albright became the first female secretary of state in 1997. By 2009, women comprised only 15 percent of Congress, despite making up over half the U.S. population. Those who were in Congress continued to make important strides, including Nancy Pelosi, who became the first female Speaker of the House in 2007.

In 1993, President Bill Clinton appointed Hillary to head the Task Force on National Health Care Reform.

She would continue to work on health care reform as a senator, and promised to address the issue if she were elected president.

DEPARTMENT OF STATE
UNITED STATES OF AMERICA

A New Political Force

As a senator, Hillary continued to advocate for health care reform, lamenting that the insurance system was incompatible with technological advances like genetic testing. "Knowing you are prone to cancer or heart disease or Lou Gehrig's disease may give you a fighting chance," she said. "But just try, with that information in hand, to get health insurance in a system without strong protections against discrimination for pre-existing or genetic conditions."

She also took a jab at those who had blocked the health care reform recommended by the task force during Clinton's administration. "In 1993, the critics predicted that if the Clinton administration's universal health care coverage plan became law, costs would go through the roof. *Hospitals will have to close,* they said. *Families will lose their choice of doctors. Bureaucrats will deny medically necessary care.*

"They were half right. All that has happened. They were just wrong about the reason.

"In 1993, there were 37 million uninsured Americans . . . now some 43.6 million Americans are uninsured, and the vast majority of them are in working families. In 1993, forty-six percent of companies with 500 or more employees offered some type of retiree health benefit. That declined to 29 percent in 2001."[1]

But she also acknowledged the task force had contributed to its own failure by making mistakes and perhaps trying to do too much too fast. "I learned some valuable lessons about the legislative process, the importance of bipartisan cooperation and the wisdom of taking small steps to get a big job done."[2]

Those who assumed Hillary would push a far-left political agenda in the Senate were surprised when she positioned herself as a centrist. While still

President William Jefferson Clinton, First Lady Hillary Rodham Clinton, and daughter Chelsea Clinton on parade on Inauguration Day, January 20, 1997. Chelsea was sixteen years old when her father began his second term as president.

pro-choice, she supported sex education and pregnancy prevention, summing up her position by saying abortion should be safe, legal, and rare. She called for more vigilant border security and a system to track immigrants—but also cosponsored a bill to give illegal agricultural workers amnesty. She supported another bill that proposed giving permanent-resident status to illegal immigrants who had been in the country for at least five years and worked for at least two years.

Hillary also made a point to become better versed in national defense issues, an area in which she had little experience. In college, she had protested against the war in Vietnam, but in the Senate she became a vocal ally of the military and supported maintaining a strong U.S. military presence internationally. In 2002, she was recruited by the Senate Democratic leadership to serve on the powerful Armed Services Committee, making her the first Senator from New York of either party to serve on that particular committee. She emerged as a staunch supporter of the military, arguing against base closures, proposing pay raises for soldiers, and lobbying for improved health benefits for the National Guard.

Her growth as a legislator, along with her savvy at building consensus with Republicans, earned Hillary newfound respect from former political adversaries. It also increased suspicions among Democrats and Republicans alike that she was poising herself for higher office. While campaigning for reelection to the Senate in 2006, Hillary was regularly asked if she would leave the Senate to run for president. She deflected such speculations, saying she was focused on representing the people of New York.

New Yorkers overwhelmingly reelected Clinton, even though the majority of those polled believed she would run for president. As it turned out, they were right. In January 2007, just two months after her reelection and ten days after Illinois Senator Barack Obama announced his intention to establish a presidential exploratory committee, Hillary announced her intention to run for president. The announcement, posted on her web site, was the simple statement: "I'm in."[3]

With those two words, she was on track to make history. Should she win the run for president, she would be the country's first female president, not to mention the first former First Lady to do so. But Clinton wasn't the only one with the potential to make history. Another candidate, New Mexico Governor Bill Richardson, would be the first Hispanic president if he won. And Barack Obama was looking to be the first African American elected to the nation's highest office. The other Democrats vying for the party's nomination were Senator John Edwards of North Carolina, Representative Dennis Kucinich of Ohio, Iowa Governor Tom Vilsack, Senator Joe Biden of Delaware, Connecticut Senator Christopher Dodd, and Alaska Senator Mike Gravel.

Of the Democratic nominees, the fifty-nine-year-old Clinton was the immediate front-runner. She said her priorities as president would be affordable health care, making the United States energy independent, reducing the deficit, and ending the war in Iraq. "After six years of George Bush, it is time to renew

When Clinton officially announced her intention to run for president, she invited voters to communicate with her. "Let's start a dialogue about your ideas and mine, because the conversation in Washington has been just a little one-sided lately."[4]

the promise of America," she said in her announcement video. "I grew up in a middle-class family in the middle of America, and we believed in that promise. I still do. I've spent my entire life trying to make good on it, whether it was fighting for women's basic rights or children's basic health care, protecting our social security or protecting our soldiers."[5]

Senator Obama welcomed her announcement and said in a statement: "Senator Clinton is a good friend and a colleague whom I greatly respect. I welcome her and all the candidates, not as competitors, but as allies in the work of getting our country back on track."[6]

Not only had her constituents in New York been right about her running for president, they would also prove prescient in their belief that Hillary would be treated more harshly than her competitors in a campaign for the White

House. And not just over her experience or political track record—her looks became an issue. In December 2007, Matt Drudge posted on his news web site an unflattering photograph of Clinton titled *The Toll of a Campaign,* in which she looks markedly older than usual. Conservative radio talk show host Rush Limbaugh asked his listeners, "So the question is this: will this country want to actually watch a woman get older before their eyes on a daily basis? . . . Men aging makes them look more authoritative, accomplished, distinguished. Sadly, it's not that way for women, and they will tell you."

Hillary in particular, he said, "is not going to want to look like she's getting older, because it will impact poll numbers, it will impact perceptions . . . there will have to be steps taken to avoid the appearance of aging. . . . Let me give

As the primary season began, there were eight hopefuls vying for the Democratic nomination. In addition to Clinton, the candidates included Senator Joseph Biden, Senator Christopher Dodd, Governor Bill Richardson, Senator Barack Obama, former Senator John Edwards, Representative Dennis Kucinich, and former Senator Mike Gravel.

you a picture, just to think about: the campaign is Mitt Romney vs. Hillary Clinton in our quest in this country for visual perfection, hmm?"[7]

At various times she was criticized for the pitch of her voice, questioned over her likability, and heckled by men asking her to iron their shirts. *Los Angeles Times* columnist Meghan Daum believed that likability was completely tied to gender. She wrote: "For a lot of people, Hillary Clinton just wants this too badly. Her Achilles heel is . . . that she is visibly salivating from hunger. That may be OK for male candidates, whose appetites tend to be selling points. But if there's anything that's drilled into women's heads before we're old enough to even ask for something, it's the importance of playing hard to get, of pretending we don't want anything at all."[8]

Vogue editor-in-chief Anna Wintour was dismayed at the media's double standard in dealing with Clinton, which in turn forced Hillary to be on constant guard about gender-related concerns. Wintour wrote: "Imagine my amazement . . . when I learned that Hillary Clinton, our only female presidential hopeful, had decided to steer clear of our pages at this point in her campaign for fear of looking too feminine. The notion that a contemporary woman must look mannish in order to be taken seriously as a seeker of power is frankly dismaying. How has our culture come to this? How is it that *The Washington Post* recoils from the slightest hint of cleavage on a senator? This is America, not Saudi Arabia. It's also 2008: [former British Prime Minister] Margaret Thatcher may have looked terrific in a blue power suit, but that was 20 years ago. I do think Americans have moved on from the power-suit mentality, which served as a bridge for a generation of women to reach boardrooms filled with men. Political campaigns that do not recognize this are making a serious misjudgment."[9]

Having to deal with this added pressure on top of the strain of the campaign is part of what prompted Hillary's display of emotion in the days leading up to the New Hampshire primary. After being named the front-runner by the media when she announced her candidacy, she suffered a sobering loss in the Iowa caucuses and was expected to lose in New Hampshire. But her stunning comeback put her campaign back on track and gave Hillary a newfound sense of determination. She promised her supporters she would fight all the way to the convention—but few realized the nomination would ultimately hinge on the opinions of just 800 people.

Most states choose delegates for the national presidential conventions by holding primary elections that determine which candidate receives that state's delegates. There are two kinds of primaries: In an open primary, all registered voters can vote for any candidate, regardless of their political party. In a closed primary, voters may vote only for candidates representing their registered party.

The popularity of primaries is relatively new. Earlier in the nation's history, all states chose delegates by caucuses. Amid accusations of corruption in the 1970s, caucuses began to fall out of favor. By 1980, over 70 percent of delegates for the national conventions were selected by primary elections.

In general, a caucus is an informal meeting of members of a political party. They meet in small, separate gatherings in towns and neighborhoods across the state to decide which candidate to support. Caucuses can be run in several different ways. In Iowa, for example, Republicans from each of the state's 1,784 voting precincts gather to discuss the candidates, then they vote by secret ballot to determine the winner. Democrats separate into groups supporting the individual candidates, then engage in a debate to try to get others to join their side. Any group that doesn't have a certain percentage of participants must disband, and those people have to join one of the remaining groups. Instead of being a winner-take-all state, Iowa delegates are eventually split proportionally among the candidates once the caucus process is finished.

Like New Hampshire, Iowa is the focus of national media attention during presidential election years because its caucuses are considered an early litmus test for each candidate's popularity, and a strong showing can establish an early front-runner. On the other hand, a dismal result will usually prompt a candidate to drop out of the race.

Critics of this system complain that a small state such as Iowa does not represent America as a whole as far as ethnicity, race, and socioeconomic status. Therefore it can have a disproportionate influence on the overall nomination process.

IOWA 2008 DEMOCRATIC PRESIDENTIAL CAUCUSES			
CANDIDATE	**Precinct Delegates**	**Percentage**	**Estimated National Delegates**
Barack Obama	940	37.58%	16
John Edwards	744	29.75%	14
Hillary Clinton	737	29.47%	15
Bill Richardson	53	2.11%	0
Joe Biden	23	0.93%	0
Christopher Dodd	1	0.02%	0
Mike Gravel	0	0.00%	0
Dennis Kucinich	0	0.00%	0
Uncommitted	3	0.14%	0
Total	2,501	100.00%	45

On March 31, 2008, Hillary Clinton (right) appeared on *Saturday Night Live* with Amy Poehler, a comedian who impersonates her.

To reach a broader audience, candidates appeared on less formal television shows than they had in the past, such as Saturday Night Live, The Daily Show with Jon Stewart, *and* Late Show with David Letterman.

Down to the Wire

When Americans vote for a mayor or a governor or a senator, the candidate with the most votes wins. Those officials are elected directly by citizens. The process for electing a president is very different. It's not the popular vote that counts; it's the Electoral College votes. The process for selecting the nominees is also indirect, so finding the winner is not simply a matter of tallying the votes in the primaries and caucuses. Delegates actually choose the nominee. To become the Democratic nominee, Hillary needed to secure 2,025 delegate votes. When people voted during the primary, what they really determined was which candidate their state's delegates would support at the Democratic convention.

However, there is a significant number of other delegates, mostly party leaders and elected officials, who are free to vote for any candidate they want, regardless of the popular vote of their state. These are called superdelegates, and they came into existence as a kind of compromise. Until the 1970s, nominees for president were selected by officials from the Republican and Democratic parties. Then primaries and caucuses gave citizens a voice in saying who they wanted to run. But officials still wanted to have a say in the final decision, so the superdelegate, also called unpledged delegate, was created in 1982. As superdelegates, active politicians would have a greater role in presidential elections.

Meredith McGehee, policy director for the Campaign Legal Center in Washington, D.C., explained that after Richard Nixon's landslide victory over George McGovern in 1972, "There was a view that the Democratic party had allowed the grass roots to become too empowered and that in too many instances, people whose job it was to get Democrats elected were being shut out of the process."[1]

In 2008, Democrats had 796 superdelegates, comprised of all Democratic members of Congress, the Democratic governors, members of the Democratic National Committee, and other elected officials. Counting the superdelegates, there was a total of 4,049 available delegates. To win the nomination, Hillary or Obama needed to secure 2,025 delegate votes. Normally, there's a relatively rapid attrition of candidates and a clear winner emerges long before the national convention. In those cases, the role of the superdelegates isn't that important. But in a close race, they can determine who wins. Many people feel that using superdelegates is not compatible with true democratic ideals because super-delegates do not have to follow the will of the people.

The race between Clinton and Obama was one of the closest in history. The campaigns had two very different strategies. Obama's strategy was to spend as much time in small states with fewer delegates, while Clinton concentrated on the most populous states such as California, Pennsylvania, Florida, Texas, and Ohio. Their respective wins reflected those strategies. On Tuesday, February 5, 2008, twenty-two states held Democratic primaries or caucuses. Hillary won 9 of the 22 primaries, collecting 834 delegates, while Obama took 13 states for a total of 847 delegates. It was like watching a boxing match—Clinton landing big roundhouse punches and Obama countering with relentless jabs, with both racking up nearly identical numbers of delegates.

By Super Tuesday, Hillary was struggling with another disadvantage: her campaign was almost broke while Obama's was flush. His huge cash flow advantage helped Obama reel off eleven straight victories, many in the smaller caucus states Hillary had either ignored or didn't have the money to canvass.

Despite the financial disadvantage and Obama's momentum, Hillary remained publicly upbeat. She did not show her vulnerable side as she had in New Hampshire. "I am good. I am great. I'm having a terrific time. I mean, from the outside, campaigns look as hectic and grueling as they are, but on the inside it's a really intimate experience in a lot of ways. You feel like you're invited into people's lives in a way that is very precious to me."[2]

Campaigning could also be a minefield. While campaigning for Hillary in South Carolina, Bill Clinton upset some voters by suggesting that people were supporting either Hillary or Obama based on gender or race. "As far as I can tell, neither Senator Obama nor Hillary have lost votes because of their race or gender," he said. "They are getting votes, to be sure, *because* of their

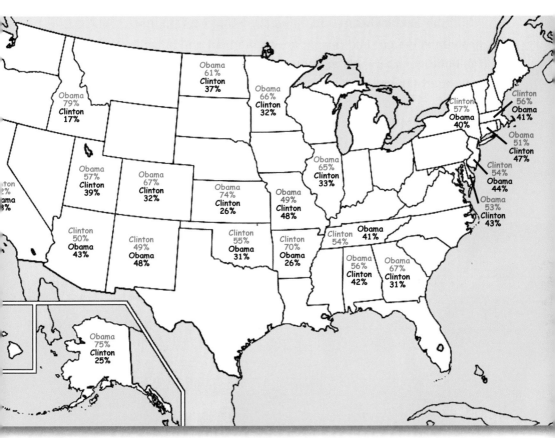

On Super Tuesday, twenty-two states held Democratic primaries or caucuses. Clinton won 9 of them, including New York and California. She collected 577 delegates that day, for a total of 834, while Obama took 13 states and 561 delegates, for a total of 847.

race or gender—that's why people tell me Hillary doesn't have a chance of winning here." He added that voting for president along racial and gender lines "is understandable, because people are proud when someone who they identify with emerges for the first time."[3]

Hillary downplayed her husband's comments. "Well, I think he is a very passionate promoter and defender of me, and I appreciate that," she said. "I think we all have spouses who are totally committed to our candidacies. But this campaign is about me. It's about what kind of president I will be, what I will do as president. So, I want everyone who is supporting me to be on the same page about that."[4]

She acknowledged that emotions were running high. "We're in a very heated campaign, and people are coming out and saying all kinds of things. I'm out there every day making a positive case for my candidacy. I have a lot of wonderful people, including my husband, who are out there making the case for me."[5]

Some of Hillary's supporters, though, wanted her to address the gender issue head on. She finally discussed it during an appearance on *Nightline*. "I think a lot of women project their own feelings and their lives on to me. And they see how hard this is. It's hard. It's hard being a woman out there. It is obviously challenging with some of the things that are said, that are not even

During the primaries, there were several debates among all the Democratic candidates—but by the end of January 2008, Obama and Clinton were the only two candidates left. Obama presented himself as the candidate for change, while Hillary stressed her superior experience.

Clinton, next to North Carolina Governor Mike Easley, speaks to a crowd from the bed of a pickup. As the race between Clinton and Obama continued into May, more superdelegates decided to endorse Obama, but Clinton continued to draw the popular vote.

personal to me as much as they are about women. And I think women just sort of shake their heads. My friends do. They say, *Oh, my gosh, this is so hard.* Well, it's supposed to be hard. I'm running for the hardest job in the world."[6]

As the primary season progressed into May, it was clear the Democratic Party was almost evenly split between Hillary and Obama. Through May 21, counting all states that held primaries, Hillary had amassed 17,172,328 popular votes to Obama's 16,881,493, but Obama held slightly more delegates. The Democratic nomination would come down to the superdelegates.

After winning Ohio, Texas, and Pennsylvania, Clinton believed she had made a stronger case for the superdelegate votes, even as some members of the Democratic National Committee suggested anonymously in the media that she was hurting the party's chance of winning the general election by not conceding to Obama. Hillary dismissed the complaints, convinced she was in a better position to beat John McCain, the Republican nominee.

"This is just idle talk," she said in late May. "You have to know how to run a campaign that's going to win. I mean, you put my base against my opponent's base, mine's much broader and deeper. And I think that's what's going to matter. When people start asking themselves, who's our better candidate, who can we actually put up against John McCain, you know, it is who can better win, and I've won the big states. I've won the states that we have to anchor. If we had the Republican rules, I would already be the nominee."[7] (The Republican superdelegate process is different than the Democratic process.)

The Clinton campaign was especially upset at the committee's decision concerning the Florida and Michigan delegates. Neither candidate campaigned in Florida or Michigan. Hillary carried those two states, but the Democratic National Committee ruled it would not count delegates from either one because their primaries were scheduled too early. In Michigan, Obama did not put his name on the ballot, so Hillary's side insisted Obama should not get any of the 73 pledged delegates, and that she should get all those plus the 55 who were uncommitted. Obama's side insisted the only fair solution would be to split the delegates in half, with 64 each. Democratic Party officials decided on a compromise: Clinton would take 69 delegates and Obama 59. Each delegate would get half a vote at the convention.

They also agreed to seat the Florida delegation based on the outcome of the January primary, with 105 pledged delegates for Clinton and 67 for Obama. Again, each delegate would get half a vote as a penalty.

With this resolution, each candidate needed 2,118 votes to clinch the nomination. Hillary's only hope was to convince the superdelegates that she was the more electable candidate before time ran out.

The presidency is the only political office not determined by popular vote. Instead, Americans choose presidents by means of an indirect election through the Electoral College. The term *college* in this case refers to a group of people who act together as a group, such as to elect a president. This system was established by the founding fathers as a compromise between letting citizens elect a president by popular vote or giving the responsibility to Congress.

While it may seem fairer to choose a president by popular vote, the crafters of the Constitution wanted to ensure that the influence of less populated states would not be overshadowed by more populated states. The Electoral College would ensure that a candidate won in a cross section of states, not just in one area of the country.

The Constitution gives each state legislature the freedom to designate a method of choosing electors. The number of electors is equal to the number of representatives and senators the state has in Congress. All but two states—Maine and Nebraska—are winner-take-all. Since 1964 there have been a total of 538 electors, so a candidate must amass 270 electoral votes to be elected president. Because the number of electoral votes varies by state, it is possible for a candidate who loses the popular vote to have more electoral votes and win the presidency. This is what happened in 2000 when George W. Bush defeated Al Gore.

Several proposals have been introduced to change the presidential election process, including using a simple majority-wins popular vote, but none have been passed by Congress.

2008 Electoral College Results

WWW.BARACKOBAMA.COM

WOMEN
for
OBAMA

Backed by a majority of superdelegates, Obama won the primary election.

Clinton officially ended her candidacy on June 7, 2008. In the months leading up to the national election, Clinton frequently campaigned for Obama.

WWW.BARACKOBAMA.COM

CHANGE
WE CAN BELIEVE IN

CHAPTER 5

One Door Closes . . .

According to national polls, both Clinton and Obama were considered likely to beat McCain in a general election as far as popular vote. But which candidate was best positioned to carry the key states necessary to ensure an Electoral College victory? Mark Penn, Clinton's senior campaign adviser, pushed for the superdelegates to entrust Hillary to appeal to a broad range of registered voters. He argued that a large percentage of Obama's declared delegates were from caucuses, which traditionally attract far fewer voters than primaries; therefore they represent a smaller cross section of voters. Hillary's victories were in primaries and in large swing states like Ohio and Pennsylvania.

"I think for superdelegates," Penn said, "the quality of where the win comes from should matter in terms of making a judgment about who might be the best general election candidate."[1]

Despite the mounting odds against her, Clinton kept fighting, a quality she credits her father for instilling in her. "My father, he was out there throwing football passes to me and teaching me to switch hit in baseball. And he just didn't see any difference between me and my brothers and all the neighborhood kids, and I've often believed that part of the reason that I can make this race for the presidency, that I can withstand all of the incoming fire, is because my dad basically believed in me, he encouraged me, he set high standards for me and he said, *Look, you have to get out there, you have to stand up for yourself, you have to find your way in the world.* And I miss him, I wish he were around, he would be just speechless, I think."[2]

Hillary continued to contend and continued to win delegates, winning Pennsylvania, Indiana, West Virginia, Kentucky, Puerto Rico, and South Dakota. But as the day of the final primaries neared, Obama was only 38 delegates shy of clinching the nomination, while Hillary needed 207. A significant majority of superdelegates opted to support Obama, even though after the last primary was tallied, Hillary carried the popular vote by a 17,616,502 to 17,272,520 margin.

Congress Daily political writer Erin McPike wrote an article explaining how the political aspirations of Democrats in Congress, all of whom are super-delegates, figure into the selection of the Democratic nominee. In her view, most candidates running for office—a third of the Senate, all of the House, and several governors—believed Obama would have bigger and stronger coattails than Hillary. And that was more important to them than the candidates' policies. She quoted Illinois Congressman Rahm Emanuel as saying, "many of our [most vulnerable House freshmen] are crossing their fingers for Obama because . . . they know he is a much less polarizing figure."[3]

Hillary supporters held out hope that if she went to the convention, she might convince the superdelegates to change their minds. That was the last thing Democratic Party officials wanted. They wanted to present a unified front at the national convention. And if Hillary was anything, it was a team player. She did not want to do anything that would jeopardize the chance for Democrats to win the White House. In early June, Hillary gave the first indications that she was preparing to concede. Some suspected she was delaying her concession for leverage in an effort to be named Obama's running mate. On June 3, 2008, the *Times Online* reported: "in a conference call with other New York senators, she was asked by Democratic representative Nydia Velázquez whether the best way for Mr. Obama to win over key voting blocs, including Hispanics, would be for him to choose Mrs. Clinton as his running mate. She replied: 'I am open to it,' if it would help the party's prospects in November's presidential elections against John McCain."[4]

Some pundits, however, doubted Hillary would want to be vice president, seen by many as a thankless, mostly invisible position. The speculation would continue throughout the summer up to the convention.

On June 7, 2008, Hillary Clinton formally conceded in Washington, D.C., and endorsed Barack Obama. "Well, this isn't exactly the party I'd planned, but I sure like the company," she told her supporters, many of whom wept.

"I want to start today by saying how grateful I am to all of you . . . who invested so much in our common enterprise, to the moms and dads who came

Clinton's defeat was a bitter blow to her followers. Some were angry at Democratic officials who backed Obama despite Hillary winning the popular vote. Despite being disappointed at not winning the nomination, Clinton publicly endorsed Obama and urged her supporters to do the same.

to our events, who lifted their little girls and little boys on their shoulders and whispered in their ears, 'See, you can be anything you want to be . . .'

"To all those women in their 80s and their 90s born before women could vote who cast their votes for our campaign . . . To all those who voted for me, and to whom I pledged my utmost, my commitment to you and to the progress we seek is unyielding. You have inspired and touched me with the stories of the joys and sorrows that make up the fabric of our lives and you have humbled me with your commitment to our country."[5]

She thanked everyone who voted for her, saying they reaffirmed her commitment to fight for affordable health care and remain an advocate for women and children.

"I entered this race because I have an old-fashioned conviction: that public service is about helping people solve their problems and live their dreams. I've had every opportunity and blessing in my own life and I want the same for all Americans. Until that day comes, you will always find me on the front lines of democracy, fighting for the future . . .

"Think how much progress we have already made. When we first started, people everywhere asked the same questions: Could a woman really serve as Commander-in-Chief? Well, I think we answered that one. And could an African American really be our President? Senator Obama has answered that one. Together Senator Obama and I achieved milestones essential to our progress as a nation, part of our perpetual duty to form a more perfect union."[6]

Although Hillary strongly expressed her endorsement for Obama, many of her supporters resisted throwing their support to Obama, with some suggesting they might vote for McCain out of protest. But she reiterated her support at the Democratic convention in August. "Whether you voted for me, or voted for Barack, the time is now to unite as a single party with a single purpose. We are on the same team, and none of us can sit on the sidelines. This is a fight for the future. And it's a fight we must win . . .

"I haven't spent the past 35 years in the trenches advocating for children, campaigning for universal health care, helping parents balance work and family, and fighting for women's rights at home and around the world . . . to see another Republican in the White House squander the promise of our country and the hopes of our people. . . . Barack Obama is my candidate. And he must be our President."[7]

The speculation about Hillary being Obama's running mate ended when Joe Biden was named the vice presidential nominee. Even then, Hillary remained highly visible, campaigning for Obama and encouraging her supporters to give him their vote. In the end, most did, and on November 4, 2008, Barack Obama became the first African American elected president.

While Hillary may not have been selected Obama's running mate, his win still resulted in a surprising new opportunity. Just weeks after the election, on December 1, Obama named Hillary Clinton to be his secretary of state. In

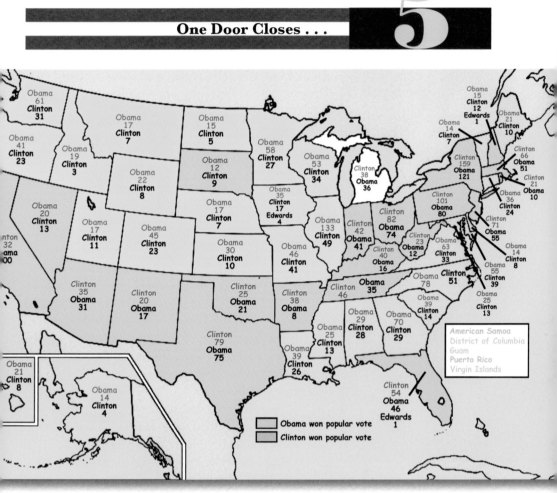

The winner of the popular vote in a state did not necessarily win the state's delegate vote. Clinton won the large delegate-rich states and the overall popular vote; Obama won the smaller states and the backing of the superdelegates. In Michigan, Obama was not on the ballot, but the delegates there were able to vote.

his announcement, he said about her: "She possesses an extraordinary intelligence and toughness, and a remarkable work ethic. . . . She is an American of tremendous stature who will have my complete confidence, who knows many of the world's leaders, who will command respect in every capital, and who will clearly have the ability to advance our interests around the world."[8]

The news was greeted with bipartisan support and international excitement and opened the door to a new chapter in what is already a storied and unprecedented life of public service.

The secretary of state is the head of the United States Department of State, the organization that oversees foreign affairs. The secretary is the country's top diplomat, serving as the president's primary spokesperson on foreign policy. The secretary is also the highest ranking member of the president's cabinet, and under law is a member of the National Security Council. The secretary of state is fourth in line to the presidency, behind the vice president, Speaker of the House of Representatives, and president pro tempore of the Senate.

The Constitution gives the president the responsibility and authority to direct America's foreign policy. But rather than have the president conduct diplomacy directly, in July 1789 the House of Representatives and Senate approved legislation for George Washington to establish a Department of Foreign Affairs (this was the first federal agency to be created under the new Constitution). Later that year, the agency was renamed the Department of State.

Among the original responsibilities assigned to the Department of State were domestic duties such as taking the national census, managing the U.S. Mint, preserving laws, and taking custody of the Great Seal of the United States and of the records of the Continental Congress, including the Constitution and the Declaration of Independence. During the nineteenth century, other federal agencies were established to handle most of those duties, leaving the State Department to focus primarily on foreign affairs. As secretary of state, Clinton would supervise the State Department's activities and offices overseas, including consulates and embassies. She would negotiate with foreign leaders and governments on behalf of the president and advise Obama on foreign policy.

It is ironic that many political pundits commented that taking the secretary of state position would undermine any future presidential aspirations Hillary Clinton might have, because in the early years of the country, being named secretary of state was considered a natural stepping-stone to being elected president. Among the secretaries of state who went on to the presidency were Thomas Jefferson, James Madison, James Monroe, John Quincy Adams, Martin Van Buren, and James Buchanan. Whether or not Hillary Clinton will be added to that list remains to be seen.

Chapter Notes

Chapter 1. The Comeback Kid
 1. Cynthia McFadden and Melinda Arons, "Hillary Clinton's Campaign: A Look Back," *Nightline*, June 2, 2008 http://abcnews.go.com/Nightline/Vote2008/Story?id=4983093&page=1
 2. Howard Kurtz, "For Clinton, A Matter of Fair Media," *Washington Post*, December 19, 2007 C01, http://www.washingtonpost.com/wp-dyn/content/article/2007/12/18/AR2007121802184_pf.html
 3. Ibid.
 4. John F. Harris and Jim Vandehei, "Why Reporters Get It Wrong," *Politico*, January 9, 2008, http://www.politico.com/news/stories/0108/7822_Page2.html
 5. Philip Elliott. "Clinton Trying Not to 'Fall Backwards.'" *Associated Press*, January 8, 2008 http://www.dispatchpolitics.com/live/content/national_world/stories/2008/01/08/ap_campaign_rdp.ART_ART_01-08-08_A4_Q790CN4.html?sid=101
 6. CBS, Early Show, interview, Janury 9, 2008.
 7. Live televised speech. CNN. January 8, 2008.
 8. Ibid.

Chapter 2. Early Ambitions
 1. Anne E. Kornblut, "A Mother's Strength, a Candidate's Ambition," *Washington Post*, September 23, 2007, p. A01. http://www.washingtonpost.com/wp-dyn/content/article/2007/09/22/AR2007092201175.html
 2. Ibid.
 3. Bill Dedman, "Reading Hillary Rodham's Hidden Thesis," MSNBC.com, May 9, 2007, http://www.msnbc.msn.com/id/17388372/

Chapter 3. An New Political Force
 1. Hillary Rodham Clinton, "Now Can We Talk About Health Care?" *New York Times*, April 18, 2004, http://query.nytimes.com/gst/fullpage.html?res=9A00E7DE1E38F93BA25757C0A9629C8B63&sec=health&pagewanted=all
 2. Raymond Hernandez and Patrick D. Healy, "The Evolution of Hillary Clinton," *New York Times*, July 13, 2005, http://www.nytimes.com/2005/07/13/nyregion/13hillary.ready.html?ex=1278907200&en=ca200c39b840ad53&ei=5090&partner=rssuserland&emc=rss
 3. CNN.com, "Hillary Clinton Launches White House Bid: 'I'm In,'" January 22, 2007, http://www.cnn.com/2007/POLITICS/01/20/clinton.announcement/index.html
 4. Video Transcript: Presidential Exploratory Committee Announcement, January 20, 2007, http://www.4president.org/speeches/2008/hillaryclinton2008announcement.htm
 5. Ibid.
 6. Mark Preston, "Obama Calls Clinton a 'Good Friend,'" CNN.com, January 20, 2007, http://www.cnn.com/POLITICS/blogs/politicalticker/2007/01/obama-calls-clinton-good-friend.html

 7. Maureen Dowd, "Rush to Judgment," *New York Times*, December 19, 2007, http://www.nytimes.com/2007/12/19/opinion/19dowd.html?_r=1&oref=slogin
 8. Meghan Daum, "Hillary's Gotta Have It," *Los Angeles Times*, January 12, 2008, http://www.latimes.com/news/opinion/la-oe-daum12jan12,0,3703309.column
 9. Anna Wintour, "Letter from the Editor," *Vogue*, February 2008, http://mediamatters.org/items/200801230005

Chapter 4. Down to the Wire
 1. Joannna Klonsky, "The Role of Delegates in the U.S. Presidential Nominating Process." *Council on Foreign Relations*, June 10, 2008, http://www.cfr.org/publication/15414/
 2. Cynthia McFadden and Melinda Arons, "Hillary Clinton's Campaign: A Look Back," *Nightline*, June 2, 2008 http://abcnews.go.com/Nightline/Vote2008/Story?id=4983093&page=1
 3. Melissa Haneline, "Bill Clinton Says Race, Gender to Decide S.C. Vote" USAToday.com, January 24, 2008, http://www.usatoday.com/news/politics/election2008/2008-01-24-sc-bill-clinton_N.htm
 4. McFadden and Arons.
 5. "Bill Clinton Defends His Attacks on Obama," *Los Angeles Times*, January 25, 2008, http://articles.latimes.com/2008/jan/25/nation/na-campaign25
 6. McFadden and Arons.
 7. Ibid.

Chapter 5. One Door Closes . . .
 1. Susan Duclos, "How Your Votes Compare to Super Delegates' in the Battle Between Clinton and Obama," *Digital Journal*, February 14, 2008. http://www.digitaljournal.com/article/250324/How_Your_Votes_Compare_to_Super_Delegates_in_the_Battle_Between_Clinton_and_Obam
 2. Cynthia McFadden and Melinda Arons, "Hillary Clinton's Campaign: A Look Back." *Nightline*, June 2, 2008, http://abcnews.go.com/Nightline/Vote2008/Story?id=4983093&page=4
 3. "Many Superdelegates—Members of Congress—Praying Obama Wins By TKO on Tuesday," March 3, 2008, http://downwithtyranny.blogspot.com/2008/03/many-superdelegates-members-of-congress.html
 4. "Hillary Clinton Camp Hints at End to Presidential Bid," *Times Online*, June 3, 2008, http://www.timesonline.co.uk/tol/news/world/us_and_americas/us_elections/article4059739.ece
 5. CNN, June 7, 2008.
 6. Ibid.
 7. CNN, August 26, 2008.
 8. Liz Sidoti, "Obama Announces Clinton, Gates for Cabinet," Associated Press, December 1, 2008.

Clinton Chronology

1947	Hillary Rodham is born October 26 in Park Ridge, Illinois
1964	She campaigns for Barry Goldwater
1965	Enrolls in Wellesley College
1969	Graduates from Wellesley; enrolls in Yale Law School
1973	Meets William Jefferson Clinton at Yale; graduates with honors
1974	Serves on Nixon impeachment inquiry staff of House Judiciary Committee
	Moves to Bill Clinton's home state of Arkansas as he pursues his political career
1975	Marries Bill Clinton on October 11
1978	Appointed by President Jimmy Carter to the board of the Legal Services Corporation
1980	Daughter Chelsea is born February 27 in Little Rock, Arkansas
1983	Named Arkansas' Woman of the Year
1984	Named Arkansas' Young Mother of the Year
1988	Named one of America's 100 Most Influential Lawyers
1991	Named one of America's 100 Most Influential Lawyers a second time
1993	Becomes First Lady when husband Bill Clinton is inaugurated
	Leads national task force to reform health care
2000	Elected to U.S. Senate in New York
2002	Recruited to serve on the powerful Armed Services Committee
2003	Publishes memoir of her White House years, called *Living History*
2006	Reelected to the Senate, earning 67 percent of the vote
2007	Announces candidacy for president in January
2008	Concedes nomination to Barack Obama on June 7
	On December 1, she is nominated as secretary of state in Obama's cabinet

Chronology of the Primaries

2007

January 20	Senator Hillary Rodham Clinton announces her candidacy for president.
February 10	Senator Barack Obama announces his candidacy.

2008

January 3	Clinton places third in the Iowa Democratic caucus, behind Obama and John Edwards; Chris Dodd and Joe Biden drop out of the Democratic race.
January 8	Clinton wins New Hampshire Democratic primary; the Republican primary is won by John McCain.
January 29	Clinton wins the Florida primary by 17 points.
January 30	Former New York Mayor Rudy Giuliani withdraws from the Republican race; John Edwards drops out of the Democratic race.
February 5	Twenty-two Democratic primaries are held on Super Tuesday; Clinton wins 9 of 22 states, including California.
February 10	Clinton's campaign manager Patti Solis Doyle resigns and is replaced by Maggie Williams.

March 4	Clinton wins Rhode Island, Ohio, and Texas primaries; when Mike Huckabee withdraws, John McCain becomes the presumptive Republican nominee.
April 22	Clinton wins in Pennsylvania.
May 6	Clinton loses in North Carolina but wins in Indiana.
May 11	Obama takes the lead in the superdelegate count.
May 13	Clinton wins the West Virginia primary by 41 points.
May 23	Clinton reiterates her intention to keep campaigning and refuses to concede the nomination to Obama.
May 31	The Democratic National Committee decides to give Michigan and Florida only half a vote for each delegate.
June 3	The final Democratic primaries are held; with superdelegates, Obama leads in the delegate count.
June 7	Clinton ends her candidacy and endorses Obama.
August 28	Obama accepts the Democratic Party presidential nomination.

Timeline of U.S. Elections

1792	George Washington is elected president by a unanimous vote.
1801	Thomas Jefferson is the first president inaugurated in Washington, D.C.
1832	The first Democratic convention is held in Baltimore.
1869	Wyoming Territory gives women the right to vote.
1870	The Fifteenth Amendment states that adult male citizens of all races have the right to vote.
1899	Poll taxes are introduced to prevent African Americans from voting.
1920	The Nineteenth Amendment gives women in all states the right to vote.
1924	The Indian Citizenship Act gives Native Americans the right to vote.
1944	Franklin Roosevelt becomes the only person elected to fourth term as president.
1951	The Twenty-second Amendment is ratified, limiting the president to two terms.
1964	The Twenty-fourth Amendment outlaws poll-tax requirements for federal elections.
1965	The Voting Rights Act bans all tests used to keep African Americans from voting.
1968	Democratic candidate Robert F. Kennedy is assassinated in California.
1971	The Twenty-sixth Amendment lowers the voting age from 21 to 18.
1972	Shirley Chisholm becomes the first female candidate to win a state primary.
1980	David McReynolds is the first openly gay man to run for president.
1984	Geraldine A. Ferraro is the first woman to be chosen as a running mate by a presidential candidate from a major party.
1992	Ross Perot receives nearly 20 million votes as an Independent candidate.
2000	Voting irregularities in Florida prompt calls for voting reform.
2008	Barack Obama becomes the first African American to be elected president of the United States.

Further Reading

Books

Burlingame, Jeff. *Hillary Clinton: A Life in Politics*. Berkeley Heights, N.J.: Enslow Publishers, 2008.

Driscoll, Laura, and Judith V. Wood (Illustrator). *Hillary Clinton: An American Journey*. New York: Grosset & Dunlap, 2007.

Epstein, Dwayne. *Hillary Clinton*. Farmington Hills, Mich.: Lucent Books, 2007.

Krull, Kathleen, and Amy June Bates (Illustrator). *Hillary Rodham Clinton: Dreams Taking Flight*. New York: Simon & Schuster Children's Publishing, 2008.

Wheeler, Jill C. *Hillary Rodham Clinton*. Edina, Mich.: ABDO & Daughters, 2002.

Works Consulted

"Bill Clinton Defends His Attacks on Obama." *Los Angeles Times*, January 25, 2008. http://articles.latimes.com/2008/jan/25/nation/na-campaign25

Clinton, Hillary Rodham. "Now Can We Talk About Health Care?" *New York Times*, April 18, 2004. http://query.nytimes.com/gst/fullpage.html?res=9A00E7DE1E38F93BA25757C0A9629C8B63&sec=health&pagewanted=all

CNN.com. "Hillary Clinton Launches White House Bid: 'I'm In.'" January 22, 2007. http://www.cnn.com/2007/POLITICS/01/20/clinton.announcement/index.html

CNN.com. "Obama Calls Clinton a 'Good Friend.'" January 20, 2007. http://www.cnn.com/POLITICS/blogs/politicalticker/2007/01/obama-calls-clinton-good-friend.html

Daum, Meghan. "Hillary's Gotta Have It." *Los Angeles Times*, January 12, 2008. http://www.latimes.com/news/opinion/la-oe-daum12jan12,0,3703309.column

Dedman, Bill. "Reading Hillary Rodham's Hidden Thesis." MSNBC.com, May 9, 2007. http://www.msnbc.msn.com/id/17388372/

Dowd, Maureen. "Rush to Judgment." *New York Times*, December 19, 2007. http://www.nytimes.com/2007/12/19/opinion/19dowd.html?_r=1&oref=slogin

Duclos, Susan. "How Your Votes Compare to Super Delegates' in the Battle Between Clinton and Obama." *Digital Journal*, February 14, 2008. http://www.digitaljournal.com/article/250324/How_Your_Votes_Compare_to_Super_Delegates_in_the_Battle_Between_Clinton_and_Obam

Economist, The. "The Comeback Kid, Part Two." January 10, 2008. http://www.economist.com/world/unitedstates/displaystory.cfm?story_id=10498715

Elliott, Philip. "Clinton Trying Not to 'Fall Backwards.'" *Associated Press*, January 8, 2008. http://www.dispatchpolitics.com/live/content/national_world/stories/2008/01/08/ap_campaign_rdp.ART_ART_01-08-08_A4_Q790CN4.html?sid=101

Haneline, Melissa. "Bill Clinton Says Race, Gender to Decide S.C. Vote." USAToday.com, January 24, 2008. http://www.usatoday.com/news/politics/election2008/2008-01-24-sc-bill-clinton_N.htm

Harris, John F., and Jim Vandehei. "Why Reporters Get It Wrong." *Politico*, January 9, 2008. http://www.politico.com/news/stories/0108/7822.html

Hernandez, Raymond, and Patrick D. Healy. "The Evolution of Hillary Clinton." *New York Times*, July 13, 2005. http://www.nytimes.com/2005/07/13/nyregion/13hillary.ready.html?ex=1278907200&en=ca200c39b840ad53&ei=5090&partner=rssuserland&emc=rss

Klonsky, Joannna. "The Role of Delegates in the U.S. Presidential Nominating Process." *Council on Foreign Relations*, June 10, 2008. http://www.cfr.org/publication/15414/

Kornblut, Anne E. "A Mother's Strength, a Candidate's Ambition." *Washington Post*, September 23, 2007, p. A01.

Kurtz, Howard. "For Clinton, A Matter of Fair Media." *Washington Post*, December 19, 2007, p. C01.

McFadden, Cynthia, and Melinda Arons. "Hillary Clinton's Campaign: A Look Back." *Nightline*, June 2, 2008.

"Many Superdelegates—Members Of Congress—Praying Obama Wins By TKO on Tuesday." March 3, 2008. http://downwithtyranny.blogspot.com/2008/03/many-superdelegates-members-of-congress.html

Presidential Exploratory Committee Announcement, January 20, 2007 (video transcript). http://www.4president.org/speeches/2008/hillaryclinton2008announcement.htm

Sidoti, Liz. "Obama Announces Clinton, Gates for Cabinet." Associated Press, December 1, 2008.

Times Online. "Hillary Clinton Camp Hints at End to Presidential Bid." June 3, 2008. http://www.timesonline.co.uk/tol/news/world/us_and_americas/us_elections/article4059739.ece

Wintour, Anna. "Letter from the Editor." *Vogue,* February 2008. http://mediamatters.org/items/200801230005

On the Internet

Hillary Clinton MySpace
http://www.myspace.com/hillaryclinton

Hillary Rodham Clinton, Biography
http://www.whitehouse.gov/history/firstladies/hc42.html

Official Website of Hillary Clinton for President HillaryClinton.com
http://projects.washingtonpost.com/congress/members/c001041/

U.S. Department of State
http://www.state.gov/secretary/

Glossary

attrition (uh-TRIH-shun)—A reduction in numbers.

bipartisan (by-PAR-tih-sin)—Supported by both major political parties.

candidate (KAN-dih-dayt)—A person running for political office; someone nominated for some type of honor or prize.

consensus (kun-SEN-sus)—Group agreement.

culpability (kul-puh-BIH-lih-tee)—Degree to which a person deserves blame or is guilty for an action.

delegate (DEH-leh-get)—A person acting on behalf of another; a representative to a political convention.

glass ceiling—A figurative term for the social and corporate barrier that prevents women or minorities from advancing in a company or as a professional.

litmus test—An indicator; an important factor in determining attitudes or events.

nominate (NAH-mih-nayt)—To select or recommend a person.

prescient (PREH-shunt)—Having foresight; able to anticipate correctly.

pro tempore (proh-TEM-puh-ree)—For the time being; temporary.

pundit (PUN-dit)—A professional critic whose opinions are sometimes spread by the media.

swing state—A state that is not traditionally loyal to a specific political party in a presidential election.

Index